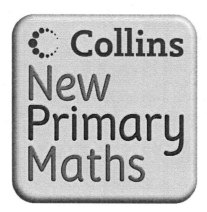

Collins New Primary Maths

Investigations 5

Developing children's investigative and thinking skills in the daily maths lesson

Peter Clarke

William Collins' dream of knowledge for all began with the publication of his first book in 1819. A self-educated mill worker, he not only enriched millions of lives, but also founded a flourishing publishing house. Today, staying true to this spirit, Collins books are packed with inspiration, innovation and practical expertise. They place you at the centre of a world of possibility and give you exactly what you need to explore it.

Collins. Freedom to teach.

Published by Collins
An imprint of HarperCollins*Publishers* Ltd.
77-85 Fulham Palace Road
Hammersmith
London
W6 8JB

Browse the complete Collins catalogue at
www.collinseducation.com

© HarperCollins*Publishers* Ltd 2009

ISBN: 978-0-00-732298-5

Peter Clarke asserts his moral right to be identified as the author of this work.

Acknowledgments
The publishers would like to acknowledge Belle Wallace's TASC Framework and the TASC Questioning Wheel which has been adapted by the author and appears on page 8 of this book as 'A model for mathematical investigations'.

The author wishes to thank Brian Molyneaux for his valuable contribution to this publication.

British Library Cataloguing in Publication Data
A Catalogue record for this publication is available from the British Library.

Cover template: Laing&Carroll
Cover illustration: Jonatronix Ltd.
Series design: Neil Adams
Illustrations: Juliet Breese

Printed by RR Donnelley at Glasgow, UK.

Contents

Introduction

Mathematical problem solving encompasses both using and applying mathematics to the solution of problems arising from the environment and reasoning and investigating questions that have arisen from within mathematics itself.

Being able to use mathematics to analyse situations and solve real-life problems is a major reason for studying the subject. Frequent use of everyday experiences will give meaning to the children's mathematical experiences. Children need to be able to apply the mathematics they have learned to real-life situations in their environment. They also need to be able to interpret and make meaning from their results. Teachers should structure situations in which children investigate problems relevant to their daily lives and relating to the recent mathematical knowledge, skills and understanding the children have acquired.

Studies of effective teachers of numeracy (Askew *et al.* 1997) have found that the most effective teachers have a 'connectionist' orientation to the teaching of mathematics. These teachers encourage children to think and talk about what they are doing and to make connections between different areas and aspects of the subject.

Collins New Primary Maths: Investigations is a series of six books for Year 1 to Year 6. It is designed to assist children in practising and consolidating the three strands of the Mathematics National Curriculum Attainment Target 1 – Using and applying mathematics: problem solving, communicating and reasoning; as well as Strand 1: Using and applying mathematics of the *Renewed Primary Framework for Mathematics* (2006). At the same time other mathematical strands are also developed such as Counting and understanding number, Knowing and using number facts, Calculating, Understanding shape, Measuring and Handling data.

Collins New Primary Maths: Investigations aims to provide teachers with a resource that enables children to:

- use and apply mathematics to solve problems arising from the environment
- reason and investigate questions that have arisen from within mathematics itself
- practise their pure mathematical knowledge and skills in an applied context
- apply their mathematical problem-solving skills in contexts that are topical, relevant and meaningful.

The activities

Collins New Primary Maths: Investigations contains two different types of activities:

Everyday problem solving

These activities include problems arising from the environment.

The activities in this section have been organised into themes. There are 12 themes, each with four different activities. The four activities can either be used together in one lesson, with different groups working on different activities, or individually over the course of a week or more.

When children solve everyday problems:

- the purpose and meaning is clear
- it is motivating

- it allows them to take control of the mathematics, choosing methods that suit them
- they are likely to feel confident about multi-tasking
- the context provides many clues and stimuli to support their thinking
- the mathematics is practical rather than abstract, and builds more obviously on children's previous experiences

Mathematical problem solving

These activities include problems arising from within mathematics itself.

When children solve mathematical problems they:

- use prior mathematical knowledge to acquire new mathematical knowledge
- make connections

Resources

- Almost all the activities in *Collins New Primary Maths: Investigations* suggest that pencil and paper be given to the children. This allows the children to feel free to work out the answers and record their thinking in ways that are appropriate to them. Giving children a large sheet of paper, such as A1, provides them with an excellent prompt to use when discussing their work, especially during the plenary. It also aids assessment for children's problem-solving, communicating and reasoning skills.

- An important problem-solving skill is to be able to identify not only the mathematics, but also what equipment to use. For this reason many of the activities do not name the specific resources that are needed. For example, in problems involving measures, the resources section states simply 'measuring equipment' to make teachers aware that a range of measuring equipment will need to be on hand for the children to choose.

- Teachers also need to be aware that some of the activities require them or the children to bring in to school resources from home.

Answers

- In the *Mathematical problem-solving* section, answers are given to the primary activities where necessary, not to the extensions .
- In the *Everyday problem-solving* section, no answers are given.

Collins New Primary Maths: Investigations and the daily mathematics lesson

The activities contained in *Collins New Primary Maths: Investigations* are ideally suited to the daily mathematics lesson. They can be used to:

- introduce new mathematical concepts using a discovery approach to teaching and learning
- consolidate children's understanding of previously taught mathematical concepts
- provide an opportunity for children to use and apply their 'pure' mathematical knowledge in more applied, problem-solving and investigative contexts
- extend the more able pupils
- challenge the 'quick finishers'

Although the activities are designed to be used by individuals, pairs or groups of children, they will be enhanced greatly if children are able to work together in pairs or groups. By working collaboratively, children are more likely to develop their problem-solving, communicating and reasoning skills.

Problem-solving skills

Collins New Primary Maths: Investigations aims to develop in children the key skills required to tackle and solve mathematical investigations.

These include:

- reading and making sense of a problem
- recognising key words, relevant information and redundant information
- finding parts of a problem that can be tackled
- recognising the mathematics which can be used to help solve a problem
- deciding which number operation(s) to perform and in which order
- choosing an efficient way of calculating
- presenting information and results in a clear and organised way
- changing measurements to the same units before calculating
- getting into the habit of checking for themselves whether the answer makes sense

Thinking skills

The National Curriculum (2000) outlines the thinking skills that complement the key knowledge, skills and understanding which are embedded in the primary curriculum.

Collins New Primary Maths: Investigations aims to develop in children these key thinking skills.

Information – processing skills
- locate, collect relevant information
- sort, classify, sequence, compare and analyse part and/or whole relationships

Reasoning skills
- give reasons for opinions and actions
- draw inferences and make deductions
- use precise language to explain what they think
- make judgements and decisions informed by reason or evidence

Enquiry skills
- ask relevant questions
- pose and define problems
- plan what to do and how to research
- predict outcomes and anticipate conclusions
- test conclusions and improve ideas

Creative thinking skills
- generate and extend ideas
- suggest hypotheses
- apply imagination
- look for alternative innovative outcomes

Evaluative skills
- evaluate information
- judge the value of what they read, hear or do
- develop criteria for judging the value of their own and others' work or ideas
- have confidence in their judgement

Problem-solving strategies

If children are actively to engage in mathematical investigations they must be taught appropriate problem-solving strategies.

Children need to be taught to:
- look for a pattern or sequence
- experiment or act out a problem
- make a drawing or model
- make a list, table or chart
- write a number sentence
- see mathematical connections
- make and test a prediction
- make a generalisation
- establish a proof
- account for all known possibilities
- solve a simpler related problem
- work backwards

A model for mathematical investigations

To be successful at solving mathematical investigations, children need to:
- be given ample opportunities to practise problem-solving skills and strategies
- work systematically and co-operatively
- use what knowledge and skills they have to help acquire new knowledge and skills
- develop self monitoring and self assessment
- talk about their work and reflect on their thinking

The model on page 8 provides children with a systematic approach to solving mathematical investigations. It also enables children to practise and develop their thinking skills.

Photocopy and enlarge this page, make it into a poster, and display it for all the class to see and follow.

Children need to be taught to use this model flexibly. They must realise that:
- not all eight stages of the model are required for every investigation
- the amount of time that is spent on each of the eight stages depends upon the nature of the investigation
- any stage in the model can be revisited at any time

A model for mathematical investigations

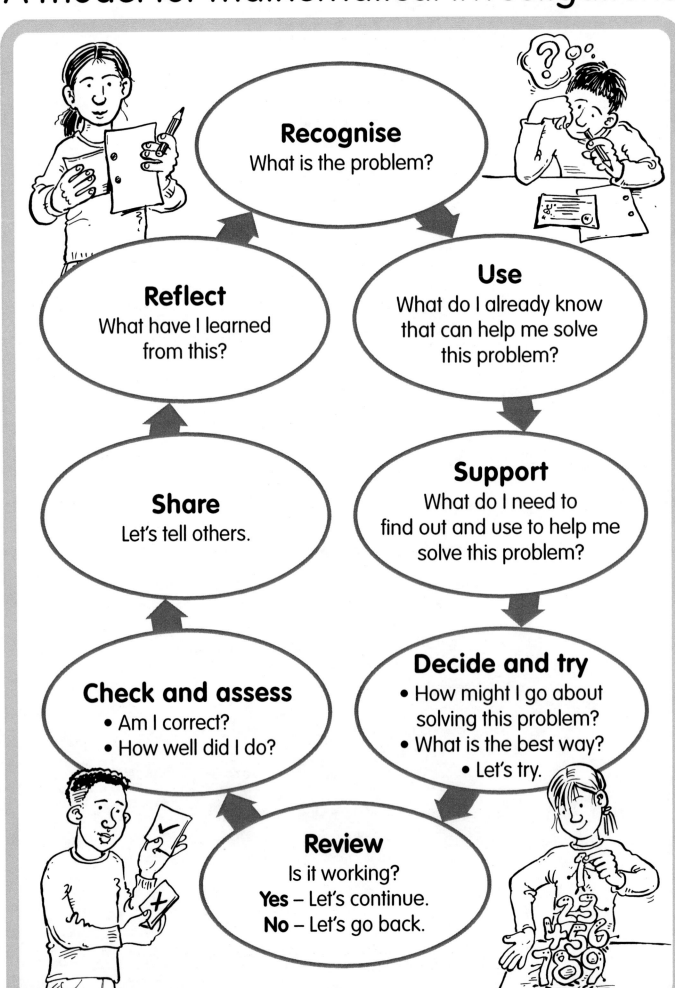

Recognise
What is the problem?

Reflect
What have I learned from this?

Use
What do I already know that can help me solve this problem?

Share
Let's tell others.

Support
What do I need to find out and use to help me solve this problem?

Check and assess
- Am I correct?
- How well did I do?

Decide and try
- How might I go about solving this problem?
- What is the best way?
- Let's try.

Review
Is it working?
Yes – Let's continue.
No – Let's go back.

Curriculum information

The activities in *Collins New Primary Maths: Investigations* are designed to improve children's attainment in the three strands of the National Curriculum Attainment Target 1 – Using and applying mathematics.

In *problem solving* by:

- using a range of problem-solving strategies
- trying different approaches to a problem
- applying mathematics in a new context
- checking their results

In *communicating* by:

- interpreting information
- recording information systematically
- using mathematical language, symbols, notation and diagrams correctly and precisely
- presenting and interpreting methods, solutions and conclusions in the context of the problem

In *reasoning* by:

- giving clear explanations of their methods and reasoning
- investigating and making general statements
- recognising patterns in their results
- making use of a wider range of evidence to justify results through logical reasoned argument
- drawing their own conclusions

The activities also provide children with an opportunity to practise and consolidate the five themes and objectives of Strand 1: Using and applying mathematics of the *Renewed Primary Framework for Mathematics* (2006):

Solving problems

- Solve one-step and two-step problems involving whole numbers and decimals and all four operations, choosing and using appropriate calculation strategies, including calculator use

Representing

- Represent a puzzle or problem by identifying and recording the information or calculations needed to solve it; find possible solutions and confirm them in the context of the problem

Enquiring

- Plan and pursue an enquiry; present evidence by collecting, organising and interpreting information; suggest extensions to the enquiry

Reasoning

- Explore patterns, properties and relationships and propose a general statement involving numbers or shapes; identify examples for which the statement is true or false

Communicating

- Explain reasoning using diagrams, graphs and text; refine ways of recording using images and symbols

In addition to these objectives, the charts on pages 10 and 11 show which other strand(s) each of the activities covers.

Everyday problem solving

These activities include problems arising from the environment.

Page	Activity	Theme	Title	1: Using and applying mathematics	2: Counting and understanding number	3: Knowing and using number facts	4: Calculating	5: Understanding shape	6: Measuring: Length (L), Mass (M), Capacity (C), Time (T), Area (A), Perimeter (P), Temperature (Temp)	7: Handling data
14	1a	Exchange rates	Local currencies	●		●	●			
14	1b		Spending abroad	●		●	●			
15	1c		Changing exchange rates	●		●	●			
15	1d		Exchange rates	●		●	●			●
16	2a	Communication	Mobile phones	●		●	●		● T	●
16	2b		Internet	●		●	●		● T	●
17	2c		Telephones	●		●	●		● T	
17	2d		News	●	●	●	●		● T	●
18	3a	Ideal house	Floor plan	●				●	● L, A, P	
18	3b		Cost of building	●		●	●		● A	
19	3c		30 m² flat	●		●	●	●	● L, A	
19	3d		Garden design	●		●	●	●	● L, A	
20	4a	Our class	Who am I?	●	●	●	●		● L, M	●
20	4b		Our grandparents	●	●	●	●			●
21	4c		A few of my favourite things	●						●
21	4d		Our birthdays	●	●		●		● T	●
22	5a	Supermarkets	'Win a Trolleyfull'	●		●	●			
22	5b		How much money?	●		●	●			●
23	5c		Supermarket receipts	●		●	●			●
23	5d		Shopping for the family	●		●	●			●
24	6a	Health and hygiene	Dental floss	●		●	●		● L	
24	6b		In the bath	●		●	●		● T	●
25	6c		Lung capacity	●					● C	
25	6d		How much energy do you use?	●		●	●			●
26	7a	Playground and school	Walking around the school	●		●	●		● L, T, P	
26	7b		Wrapping up your school	●		●	●		● L, A, P	
27	7c		All stand	●		●	●		● L	
27	7d		Plants in the playground	●		●	●			
28	8a	Mosaics	Mosaic designs	●				●	● L	
28	8b		Borders	●				●	● L	
29	8c		Creating mosaic patterns	●				●	● L	
29	8d		Your own mosaic	●				●	● L	
30	9a	Paper shapes	Enlarging a hexagonal prism	●		●	●	●	● L	
30	9b		Making an octagonal prism	●				●	● L	
31	9c		Making an octahedron	●				●	● L	
31	9d		Folding a regular octagon	●				●	● L	
32	10a	Athletics	How far can they run?	●		●	●		● L, T	
32	10b		Running ratios	●	●	●	●		● L, T	
33	10c		In the field	●		●	●		● L, W	
33	10d		The triple jump	●		●	●		● L	
34	11a	Maps	Giving directions	●				●	● L	
34	11b		Find the places	●				●	● L	
35	11c		Mapping your route to school	●				●	● L, T	
35	11d		Local bus routes	●		●	●	●	● L, T	
36	12a	Interplanetary living	Weight on other planets	●	●	●	●		● M	
36	12b		Planetary temperatures	●		●	●		● Temp	
37	12c		Flying to other planets	●		●	●		● T	
37	12d		Talking from Mars	●		●	●		● T	

Mathematical problem solving

These activities include problems arising from within mathematics itself.

Page	Activity	Title	1: Using and applying mathematics	2: Counting and understanding number	3: Knowing and using number facts	4: Calculating	5: Understanding shape	6: Measuring: Length (L), Mass (M), Capacity (C), Time (T), Area (A), Perimeter (P), Temperature (Temp)	7: Handling data
38	13	Greater than and less than	●	●					●
38	14	Zero tickets	●	●					●
39	15	Multiplication square patterns	●	●	●	●			●
39	16	Common multiples	●	●	●	●			●
40	17	Square differences	●	●	●	●			●
40	18	Factors	●	●	●	●			●
41	19	Odd and even numbers	●	●	●	●			●
41	20	Fraction families	●	●	●	●			●
42	21	Improper fractions	●	●	●	●			●
42	22	Decimal remainders	●	●	●	●			●
43	23	1 to 100 percentages	●	●	●	●			●
43	24	Ratio picture	●	●	●	●	●	● L	
44	25	Decimals that total 10	●	●	●	●			●
44	26	Running digits	●		●	●			
45	27	999	●		●	●			●
45	28	4-digit totals and differences	●	●	●	●			●
46	29	Equations	●	●	●	●			
46	30	Decimal clues	●	●	●	●			●
47	31	Opposites	●		●	●			
47	32	Multiplication patterns	●	●	●	●			●
48	33	Decimal multiplications	●	●	●	●			●
48	34	Squares and multiplications	●	●	●	●			●
49	35	Multiplying by 7	●		●	●			●
49	36	Dividing multiples	●	●	●	●			●
50	37	Divisible by 11?	●		●	●			●
50	38	Using brackets	●		●	●			●
51	39	Flow chart (1)	●		●	●			●
51	40	Flow chart (2)	●		●	●			●
52	41	Same digits different answer	●		●	●			●
52	42	Missing digits	●		●	●			
53	43	Coin percentages	●	●	●	●			
53	44	Pocket money	●		●	●			●
54	45	1 million steps	●		●	●		● L	
54	46	Sacks	●		●	●		● M	●
55	47	The air we breathe	●	●	●	●		● C, T	
55	48	When will it be?	●		●	●	●	● T	
56	49	Shape areas	●		●	●	●	● A	
56	50	Expanding polygons	●				●	● P	●
57	51	Matchstick shapes	●				●	● A, P	
57	52	Rectangles	●				●		●
58	53	Shape meanings	●	●			●		
58	54	Diagonal, intersection, region	●				●		●
59	55	How many squares?	●	●	●	●	●		●
59	56	Writing co-ordinates	●				●		
60	57	Capital rotation	●				●		●
60	58	Capital lines	●				●		●
61	59	Angle quadrilaterals	●				●		
61	60	Clock angles	●				●	● T	

Assessment and record keeping

Collins New Primary Maths: Investigations activities may be used with the whole class or with groups of children as an assessment activity. Linked to the topic that is being studied at present, *Collins New Primary Maths: Investigations* will provide you with an indication of how well the children have understood the objectives being covered as well as their problem-solving skills.

The Assessment and record keeping format on page 13 can be used to assess and level children in Attainment Target 1: Using and applying mathematics. By observing individual children while they undertake a *Collins New Primary Maths: Investigations* activity, discussing their work with them, and subsequently marking their work, you will be able to gain a good understanding of their problem-solving, communicating and reasoning skills.

Your judgements about an individual child's abilities should also take into account:

- mastery of other objectives from Strand 1: Using and applying mathematics of the *Renewed Primary Framework for Mathematics* (2006)
- performance in whole-class discussions
- participation in group work
- work presented in exercise books
- any other written evidence

Once you have decided which level 'best fits' a particular child write the child's name in the box under the appropriate level. You may wish to identify how competent a child is at that level by using the following key:

C – Becoming competent in most criteria at this level

B – Competent in most criteria at this level

A – Very competent in most criteria at this level

It is envisaged that one copy of the Assessment and record keeping format would be used for your entire class.

Attainment Target 1: Using and applying mathematics
Assessment and record keeping format

Year: _____ Class: _____

Teacher: _____

LEVEL 3

Problem solving
- Develop different mathematical approaches to a problem.
- Look for ways to overcome difficulties.
- Begin to make decisions and realise that results may vary according to the 'rule' used.
- Begin to organise work.
- Check results.

Communicating
- Discuss mathematical work.
- Begin to explain thinking.
- Use and interpret mathematical symbols and diagrams.

Reasoning
- Understand a general statement.
- Investigate general statements and predictions by finding and trying out examples.

LEVEL 4

Problem solving
- Develop own strategies for solving problems.
- Use own strategies for working within mathematics.
- Use own strategies for applying mathematics to practical contexts.

Communicating
- Present information and results in a clear and organised way.

Reasoning
- Search for solutions by trying out own ideas.

LEVEL 5

Problem solving
- Identify and obtain necessary information.
- Check results, considering whether these are sensible.

Communicating
- Show understanding of situations by describing them mathematically using symbols, words and diagrams.

Reasoning
- Draw simple conclusions.
- Give an explanation for their reasoning.

LEVEL 6

Problem solving
- Carry through substantial tasks.
- Solve complex problems by independently breaking them down into smaller, more manageable tasks.

Communicating
- Interpret, discuss and synthesise information presented in a variety of mathematical forms.
- Use writing to explain and inform diagrams.

Reasoning
- Begin to give mathematical justifications.

GENERAL COMMENTS

1a

Local currencies

• financial or travel sections of a newspaper
• pencil and paper

- Look at the exchange rates of different currencies against the pound.
- Choose ten different currencies.
- How much local currency would you get if you changed £100 in each country?
- In which country would you get the most local currency?
- In which country would you get the least local currency?

Exchange rates

	Bank BUYS	SELLS
Euro	⊥·ϽE	Ⴑ·५⊏
Australia	Ƨ· l⊏५	⊐l५५
Canada	⊥·ℓ५	l·℞Ɔ
Cyprus	Ɔ·ll₽Ɓ⊏l	५⊐Ɔ५⊏
Denmark	ll·⅃५	l℞·⊏⊏
Egypt	Ϸ·⅃Ɓ	ℤ·℞Ɓ
Hong Kong	·⊦⅃Ɓ	·l⅃Ɓ
Iceland	⅃⊏℞	℞⊏Ɛ
Indonesia	ll₽l	l⅄₽⅃
Israel	ℤl⊏	⊏⅄℞
Japan	Ƨ₽E	℞Ɓ⅄
Malta	₽⅃⊏	₽·⅂l
New Zealand	℞·⅃l	E℞⊏
Norway	५⊏⅄	⅃·⊏Ɔ

- What if you exchanged £150, £250, £300, … ?

- - - - - - - - - - ✂ - - - - - - - - - -

1b

Spending abroad

• financial or travel sections of a newspaper
• pencil and paper

- Look at the exchange rates of different currencies.
- Imagine you lived in France. How much of the local currency would you get if you visited each of the following countries and changed €100?

United States of America

Australia

Japan

Hong Kong

South Africa

Cyprus

Malta

Turkey

- What if you were from the United States of America and were visiting each of the other countries? How much would you get if you exchanged $100 in each of them?

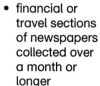

1c Changing exchange rates

- financial or travel sections of newspapers collected over a month or longer
- pencil and paper

- Look at the exchange rates of different currencies against the pound.
- Choose five different currencies.
- Investigate how their rates have changed over time against the pound.
- Do you now get more or less of these currencies for £100?
  How much more or less?

- Think about how you are going to show these changes.

1d Exchange rates

- financial or travel sections of a newspaper
- graph paper
- ruler
- pencil and paper

- Investigate the exchange rate for the pound against another currency.
- Calculate the value of £100 in that currency.
- Draw a conversion graph.

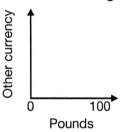

- Use the graph to calculate the value of £10, £20, £25, £50, £73, £80 in that currency.

- Investigate different currencies.

2a Mobile phones

- mobile phone tariffs
- pencil and paper

- Charles Furness needs a mobile phone. On average he makes 15 calls during the day, each lasting about 7 minutes. He also makes, on average, 4 calls an evening lasting about 12 minutes each.
- Investigate the cheapest mobile phone tariff for Charles.

- Think about different:
  - mobile phone providers
  - tariff plans.

2b Internet

- pencil and paper

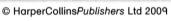

- Investigate the amount of time children in your school spend each week on the internet.
- On average, how long do children in your school spend on the internet?
- Is there a relationship between their age and the amount of time spent on the internet?

- Think about the best way to display your results.
- Don't forget to include the amount of time spent on the internet at home and at school.

2c Telephones

- telephone price guides
- pencil and paper

- Investigate the cost of making a 12 minute telephone call to someone in your local area.
- How much would a 12 minute call cost to someone in a different part of the country?
- Choose 10 different countries around the world and investigate the cost of making a 12 minute call to someone in each of these countries.

- How much difference does the time of day make to the cost of the call?
- How about making the call on different days of the week?

2d News

- television guide
- pencil and paper

One of the main ways we find out about what is happening in our local area and in the world is through news.

- Investigate the amount of time that television channels devote to news programmes.
- What percentage of time does each channel devote to news? Does this vary from one channel to another?

- Don't forget current affairs programmes.

3a Floor plan

- squared paper
- ruler
- pencil and paper

- Plan your ideal house.
- Draw a floor plan as accurately as possible.

- Think about:
  - what rooms you want to include
  - the number of floors
  - which rooms go next to each other
  - the size of each room.

3b Cost of building

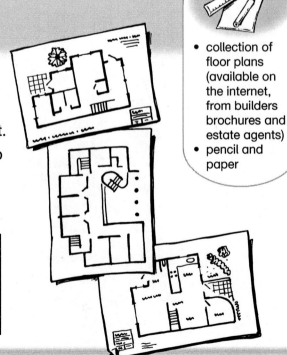

- collection of floor plans (available on the internet, from builders brochures and estate agents)
- pencil and paper

- Collect a range of floor plans for different types of houses.
- Choose the one you like the most.
- If it costs approximately £1000 to build each square metre of the house, calculate the total cost of building the house.

> **IMPORTANT**
> *If your house has more than one floor, you must include the cost of building each floor.*

- To build a luxury house it costs approximately £1600 to build each square metre. How much would it cost to build your house in this way? How much more expensive is this?

3c 30 m² flat

- squared paper
- furniture catalogues
- ruler
- pencil and paper

- Design a flat that has a total area of 30 m².
- Include the measurements of each room and all the furniture.
- Your flat must include:
  - a bedroom for two people
  - a bathroom
  - a cooking area
  - a living area.

- Think about where the windows and doors are going.
- There must be enough space around the furniture for people to move about.

3d Garden design

- squared paper
- ruler
- coloured pencils
- pencil and paper

- Design a garden for a plot of land that is 0·8 hectare in size with a house of 200 m² on it.
- Your garden must include the following features:
  - lawn
  - flower beds
  - vegetable garden.
- Include dimensions and how many square metres of each feature there are in the garden.

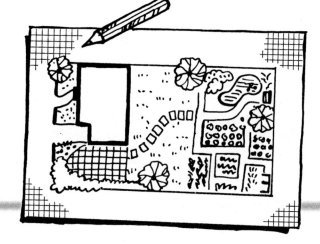

- Think about:
  - where you are going to position the house on the plot of land
  - what other features you want to include in your garden.

4a Who am I?

• measuring equipment
• pencil and paper

- Describe yourself in relation to the other children in your class so that someone else can identify you.
- You cannot describe yourself directly. That is, you cannot say your name, hair colour, eye colour, height…
- You have to describe how you are similar to, or different from, the other children in your class, but you can't name names!

I have the same shoe size as 25% of the class.
45% of the class have the same hair colour as me.
$\frac{2}{5}$ of the class have the same eye colour as me.
I'm taller than $\frac{2}{3}$ of the class.

- Think about:
  - shoe size
  - eye colour
  - hair colour
  - height
  - any other categories that are easy to measure.

4b Our grandparents

• pencil and paper

- If everyone in your class invited their grandparents to the school for Grandparents' Day, how many different nationalities / countries would be represented?
- What percentage of all the grandparents are from each country? Which is the most common country? Which is the rarest?

- How best are you going to display your results?

4c A few of my favourite things

• pencil and paper

The colour red, my bike …

My mum, Eastenders, Spain …

Chips, Christmas, …

- What are your 10 most favourite things – they can be anything!
- What about the other children in your class?
- What are the most popular favourite things in your class?

- Think about how you are going to categorise the favourite things.
- How are you going to show your results?

4d Our birthdays

• pencil and paper

- Investigate the birthdays of the children in your class.
- Predict how many children in your class were born on each day of the week.
- Now find out.
- Compare your prediction with what you have found out. Was your prediction correct? If not, why not?

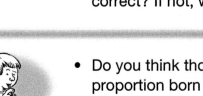

Monday's child is fair of face, Tuesday's child is …

- Do you think that the proportion born on each day would be the same if you did this for the whole school? Why? Why not?

• pencil and paper

5a 'Win a Trolleyfull'

• Imagine you are the winner of the 'Win a Trolleyfull' competition.

• You can choose anything you like from your local supermarket as long as it will fit in the supermarket trolley.

• What would you choose?

• How much would your trolleyfull be worth?

• How might this vary if an adult had won the competition?

• pencil and paper

5b How much money?

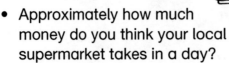

• Approximately how much money do you think your local supermarket takes in a day?

• Estimate and then find out.

• What about a week?

• Think about:
  – how much the average customer spends
  – how many tills there are
  – how many customers pass through each till
  – how much money the supermarket takes in half an hour.

5c Supermarket receipts

- supermarket receipts
- pencil and paper

- Look at a collection of supermarket receipts.
- Choose suitable categories into which you can group the items on the receipt.
- Do this for each receipt using these same categories.
- What do you notice?

- On average, which category of goods do people buy the most of? Which the least? How are you going to measure this?
- On average, which category of goods do people spend the most money on? What about the least?

5d Shopping for the family

- pencil and paper

- Imagine you are responsible for next week's shopping for your family.
- What will you buy?
- How much will this cost you?

- What if you have £20 per person per week to spend? Can you buy everything on your list with this? If not, what will you choose not to buy?

6a Dental floss

- Investigate how long a container of dental floss would last a family of four if each of them flosses once a day.

- Calculate how much they spend on dental floss in a year.

6b In the bath

I've just calculated that during my life I have spent the equivalent of 146 days in the bath.

- Could Martin be right?
- On average, how long do you think he might spend in the bath each day?
- What age do you think Martin could be?

- Calculate how much of your life you have spent in the bath or having a shower.

6c Lung capacity

- measuring equipment
- pencil and paper

An indication of how fit you are is how large your maximum lung capacity is.

- Design a device to measure lung capacity.
- Measure your lung capacity.
- Compare your lung capacity with other children in your class.

- What unit of measure will you use?

6d How much energy do you use?

- pencil and paper

- Use this table to calculate how much energy you use each day.

Activity	Calories per minute (approx)
Sleeping	0·9
Sitting	1·2
Standing	1·6
Washing and dressing	2·4
Walking slowly	2·6
Walking quickly	4·8
Running slowly	4·4
Running quickly	8·2

- Don't forget there are 24 hours in a day, have you accounted for them all?

7a Walking around the school

- measuring equipment
- pencil and paper

- What is the perimeter of your school playground?
- How long does it take you to walk around it?
- If you were trying to keep fit by walking 5 kilometres every day, how many circuits of the perimeter would you have to do?
- How long would this take you?

- How would this vary if you walked around the perimeter of the whole school?

7b Wrapping up your school

- measuring equipment
- pencil and paper

Christo is a famous artist who wraps up large buildings with fabric and rope.

MACKENZY ROAD
J & I SCHOOL

- What is the minimum amount of fabric that Christo would need to wrap up your school?

- Don't forget to wrap the roof.

7c All stand

- What is the maximum number of people that could fit into your school playground if they were all standing up?

- measuring equipment
- pencil and paper

- What if they were all lying down?
- What if they were all sitting on the ground cross-legged?

7d Plants in the playground

- Imagine your school has budgeted £200 to buy plants for your playground.
- How would you spend this money?

- gardening catalogues
- pencil and paper

- Think about:
  - the types of plants you would like to see
  - how many plants you can afford
  - if the plants will last for just one season or longer
  - where the plants are going to go
  - other things you might need to buy, apart from the plants.

8a Mosaic designs

Mosaics are decorations made from small squares of stones, metals or glass to form a design.

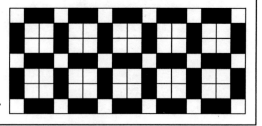

- Use this pattern to make a mosaic design.

- Now make a design using this pattern.

- What if you used this pattern?

8b Borders

Many mosaics include a repeating border pattern that is used to frame the central design.

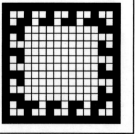

- Use this pattern to make a border.

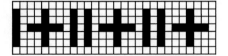

- Now make a border using this pattern.

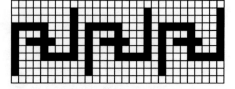

- What if you used this pattern?

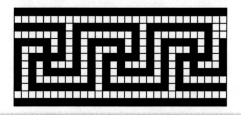

8c Creating mosaic patterns

- squared paper
- pencil
- coloured pencils

Many mosaics are created by rotating, reflecting, translating or tessellating simple shapes.

Rotating   Reflecting   Translating   Tessellating

- Using squared paper and a pencil, design your own mosaic pattern that is created from rotating shapes.
- Design another three mosaic patterns that are created from reflecting, translating and tessellating shapes.

- What if you used more than one colour in your pattern?

8d Your own mosaic

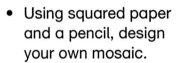

- squared paper
- pencil
- coloured pencils

- Using squared paper and a pencil, design your own mosaic.
- Make sure you include a central design and a repeating border pattern.

- What if you used more than one colour in your mosaic?

9a Enlarging a hexagonal prism

- A3 sheet of paper
- pencil
- ruler
- scissors
- glue
- sticky tape

This is the net of a hexagonal prism with sides of 18 mm.

- Enlarge this net to make the largest hexagonal prism you can using a sheet of A3 paper.
- Cut it out and make the prism.

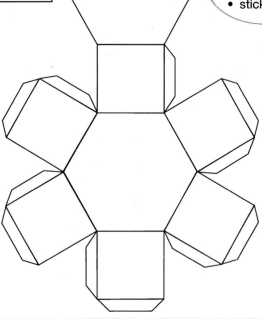

- Be sure that you are as accurate as possible or you will have gaps left around the edges of your prism.

9b Making an octagonal prism

- A3 sheet of paper
- pencil
- ruler
- scissors
- glue
- sticky tape

This is the net of a heptagonal prism.

- Draw the net of an octagonal prism on a sheet of A3 paper.
- Cut it out and make the prism.

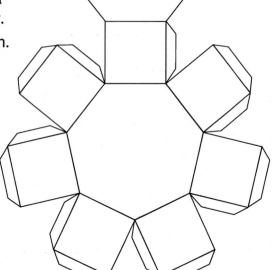

- Be sure that you are as accurate as possible or you will have gaps left around the edges of your prism.

9c Making an octahedron

- A3 sheet of paper
- pencil
- ruler
- scissors
- glue
- sticky tape

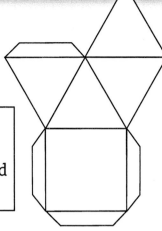

This is the net of a square-based pyramid.

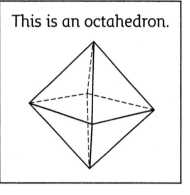

This is an octahedron.

- Using this net, can you draw the net of an octahedron?
- Cut it out and make the octahedron.

- Think about which sides of the square-based pyramid you can use.

9d Folding a regular octagon

- sheet of A4 paper

Without using any equipment I can make a regular octagon by making five folds in a sheet of A4 paper.

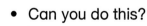

- Can you do this?

- Explain how this is possible.

10a How far can they run?

- What is the record for the 1600 m race?
- How far would the record holder run in 10 min if they ran this fast for the whole time?
- What is the record for the 100 m race?
- How far would the record holder run in 10 min if they ran this fast for the whole time?
- Is there a difference? If so, why?

Decide whether to use:
- *Olympic or World Records*
- *Men's or Women's Records*

- Estimate then find out how far the 800 m and 400 m record holders could run in 10 min.
- Plot all the results on a graph. What do you notice?

10b Running ratios

- What are the records for the 100 m race and 400 m race?
- What is the ratio between the two times?
- Now time yourself running 100 m and 400 m.
- Calculate the ratio between your two times.
- Is your ratio similar to the ratio of the record holders?
- If not, why do you think this is?

- measuring equipment
- stopwatch
- pencil and paper

Decide whether to use:
- *Olympic or World Records*
- *Men's or Women's Records*

- Compare your ratio with other children in your class.

10c In the field

- pencil and paper

- Is there a relationship between the weight of an average javelin, shot, discus and hammer, and how far each of them travels?

- Why do you think this is?

10d The triple jump

- measuring equipment
- pencil and paper

The triple jump is an athletic event where athletes hop, skip and jump.

- Try the triple jump yourself.
- Investigate what proportion of the total distance each of the three steps contributes.
- Are the proportions the same for others in your class?

- Think about how you are going to measure each of the distances.

11a Giving directions

- Ordnance Survey map or map of the local area including scale
- pencil and paper

- Using the map, plan an outing to visit five of the places shown.
- Now write directions so that a friend can visit these places in the order that you have chosen.
- You can only tell them where they start from and the directions and distances from one place to the next.
- Apart from the first place, you cannot name the places.

- Try and be as accurate as you can with your directions and distances so that your friend doesn't get lost.

11b Find the places

Collins New Primary Maths: Investigations 5

- UK map (including scale)
- pencil and paper

- Choose a city near you.
- Investigate how far, and in which direction, ten other places in the United Kingdom are from your city.

Aberdeen

Edinburgh
Glasgow
Newcastle

Belfast

Manchester
Liverpool

Cardiff
Birmingham
London
Bristol

- Be as accurate as possible so that anyone following your instructions would arrive at the right place.

11c Mapping your route to school

- measuring equipment
- squared paper
- pencil and paper

- Draw a map showing the route you travel from home to school.
- Include ten features on your map.
- Make sure that the distances on your map between each of the ten landmarks reflects the actual distances.

- Think about how you are going to measure the distances between the various landmarks:
  - by counting your steps?
  - by measuring the min / sec travelling between them?
  - using a different method?

11d Local bus routes

- local bus timetable
- map of the local area including scale
- pencil and paper

- Using a local bus timetable, draw in the bus routes on a local map.
- Investigate how long each route is in kilometres.

- Can you calculate the average speed of the bus on each route?

12a Weight on other planets

- pencil and paper

Gravity is the force that pulls things together. The bigger and heavier the planet, the greater the gravitational force. Something that weighs 10 kg on Earth would weigh 2·7 kg on Mercury, 8·6 kg on Venus, 3·7 kg on Mars and 26·4 kg on Jupiter.

- Calculate how much you would weigh on Mercury, Venus, Mars and Jupiter.

- Work out how much other objects that you might want to take with you to other planets would weigh on each of these four planets.

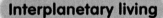

12b Planetary temperatures

- pencil and paper

- The average temperature on Earth is 22° C.
- Investigate the average temperatures on other planets in the solar system.
- Which is the hottest planet? Which is the coldest?
- How much hotter / colder are they than Earth?
- Which two planets are most similar in temperature? What is the difference in their temperatures?
- Which two planets are least similar in temperature? What is the difference in their temperatures?

- Apart from Earth, which planet would you prefer to live on? Why?

12c Flying to other planets

- If it takes a rocket 2 days and 6 hours to travel 1 million kilometres, investigate how long it would take you to travel to other planets in the solar system.

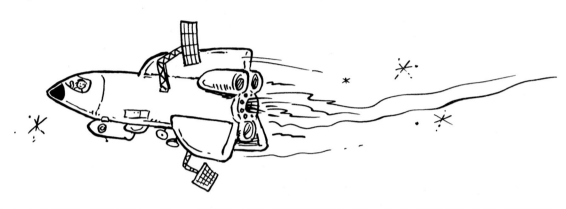

- How old would you be when you landed on each of these planets if you set off now?

12d Talking from Mars

It takes $3\frac{1}{3}$ seconds for radio waves to travel 1 million kilometres. If you said something into a radio on Mars, your friends on Earth would hear it 258 sec or 4 min 18 sec later.

- Investigate how long it would take your friends on Earth to hear you say something on other planets in the solar system.

- Choose a planet in the solar system you would like to visit. Calculate how long it would take your friends on other planets to hear you talk.

13 Greater than and less than

- 0–9 digit cards
- pencil and paper

- Shuffle a set of 0–9 digit cards.
- Deal the top six cards and place them face up on the table.

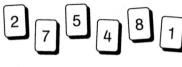

- Investigate how many different ways you can complete the statement below using the digit cards.

□□□ < □□□

2, 7, 5, 4, 8, 1
275 < 481
127 < 458

- What if the same cards were used for these statements?

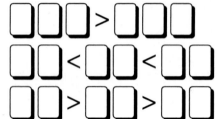

□□□ > □□□

□□ < □□ < □□

□□ > □□ > □□

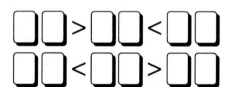

□□ > □□ < □□

□□ < □□ > □□

---

14 Zero tickets

- pencil and paper

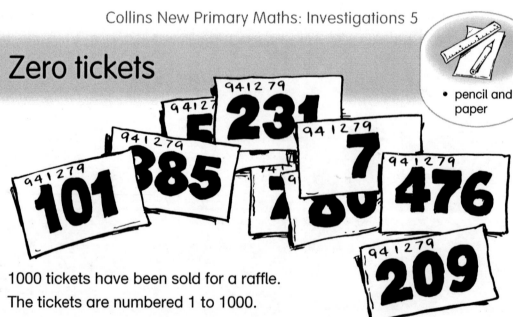

- 1000 tickets have been sold for a raffle.
- The tickets are numbered 1 to 1000.
- How many tickets have one zero? What are they?
- How many tickets have two zeros? What are they?
- How many tickets have three zeros? What are they?

- Which tickets have two or more digits the same?

15 Multiplication square patterns

- pencil and paper

- Look at any 2 × 2 square of numbers on the multiplication square.
- Add each diagonal, e.g. 12 + 20 and 15 + 16.
- Investigate other 2 × 2 squares of numbers.
- Write about what you notice.

- What if you find the sum of the 3 numbers in each diagonal of a 3 × 3 square?
- What about a 4 × 4 square?

×	1	2	3	4	5	6	7	8	9	10
1	1	2	3	4	5	6	7	8	9	10
2	2	4	6	8	10	12	14	16	18	20
3	3	6	9	12	15	18	21	24	27	30
4	4	8	12	16	20	24	28	32	36	40
5	5	10	15	20	25	30	35	40	45	50
6	6	12	18	24	30	36	42	48	54	60
7	7	14	21	28	35	42	49	56	63	70
8	8	16	24	32	40	48	56	64	72	80
9	9	18	27	36	45	54	63	72	81	90
10	10	20	30	40	50	60	70	80	90	100

16 Common multiples

- pencil and paper

- Which numbers between 1 and 100 are multiples of 4 as well as multiples of 6?
- What do you notice?

- What about multiples of 6 and multiples of 8?
- What about multiples of 3 and multiples of 5?
- What about multiples of 3 and multiples of 4?
- What about multiples of 2, 3 and 5?

1	2	3	4	5	6	7	8	9	10
11	12	13	14	15	16	17	18	19	20
21	22	23	24	25	26	27	28	29	30
31	32	33	34	35	36	37	38	39	40
41	42	43	44	45	46	47	48	49	50
51	52	53	54	55	56	57	58	59	60
61	62	63	64	65	66	67	68	69	70
71	72	73	74	75	76	77	78	79	80
81	82	83	84	85	86	87	88	89	90
91	92	93	94	95	96	97	98	99	100

17 Square differences

I can make 12 by calculating the difference between two square numbers.

$$12 = 4^2 - 2^2$$

- pencil and paper

- Investigate which numbers from 1 to 50 can be made by calculating the difference between two square numbers.

- What about finding the sum and/or difference between two or more square numbers?

---

18 Factors

- pencil and paper

The factors for **16** are 1 2 4 8 and 16

The factors for **15** are 1 3 5 and 15

- Investigate which 2-digit numbers have the most factors.
- What do you notice about these numbers?

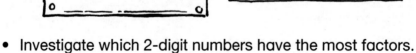

- Which 2-digit numbers have fewest factors?

19 Odd and even numbers

• pencil and paper

The sum of three even numbers is always even.

The difference between one odd and one even number is always odd.

The sum of three odd numbers is always even.

The difference between two odd or two even numbers is always odd.

• Investigate which of Natasha's statements are true.

• What about these statements?

The product of two odd numbers is always odd.

The product of two even numbers is always even.

The product of one odd and one even number is always odd.

---

20 Fraction families

• pencil and paper

$$\frac{1}{4}, \frac{2}{4}, \frac{3}{4}$$

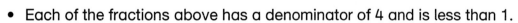

• Each of the fractions above has a denominator of 4 and is less than 1.
• Reduce each fraction to its simplest equivalent fraction.
• How many still have a denominator of 4?
• How many reduce to a denominator that is not 4?
• Investigate fraction families less than 1 with denominators of 5, 6, 7, 8, 9 or 10.
• What do you notice about the denominator in the sets where no fractions can be reduced?

• What if the denominator is greater than 10?

21 Improper fractions

• pencil and paper

This pair of improper fractions each has a denominator of 3. They also total 3.

$$\frac{6}{3} + \frac{3}{3}$$

• Investigate pairs of improper fractions with a denominator of 3 that total 4, 5, 6, 7, 8, 9, 10...

• What if the pairs of fractions each had a denominator of 5 / 6 / 7 / 8 ...?

---

22 Decimal remainders

• calculator
• pencil and paper

• Divide a 1-digit number by another 1-digit number.
• How many calculations have an answer with exactly 2 decimal places?
• What do you notice?

• How many calculations have an answer with exactly 1 decimal place?
• What if you divide a 2-digit number by a 1-digit number?
• Can you make any predictions?

23 1 to 100 percentages

• pencil and paper

- Investigate what percent of the numbers on a 1 to 100 number square are:
  - odd numbers
  - multiples of 3
  - multiples of 2 and 5
  - square numbers
  - factors of 36.

1	2	3	4	5	6	7	8	9	10
11	12	13	14	15	16	17	18	19	20
21	22	23	24	25	26	27	28	29	30
31	32	33	34	35	36	37	38	39	40
41	42	43	44	45	46	47	48	49	50
51	52	53	54	55	56	57	58	59	60
61	62	63	64	65	66	67	68	69	70
71	72	73	74	75	76	77	78	79	80
81	82	83	84	85	86	87	88	89	90
91	92	93	94	95	96	97	98	99	100

- Make up some questions that have an answer of 25%. What about 12%?
- Make up some questions that have other percentages as answers.

---

24 Ratio picture

• centimetre squared paper
• ruler
• coloured pencils
• pencil

- Using centimetre squared paper, highlight a 4 × 4 grid.
- Draw a simple picture inside the grid. Try to make sure that some part of your picture is in each of the 16 squares.
- Now enlarge your picture in the ratio of 1 : 4.

- Give the picture you have just enlarged to a friend. Ask them to reduce your picture in a ratio of 4 : 1. Compare their picture with the original picture you drew on the 4 × 4 grid.

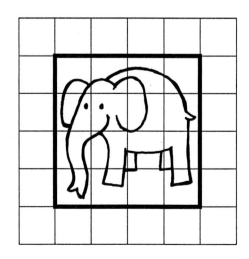

25 Decimals that total 10

• pencil and paper

$$\Box.\Box + \Box.\Box = 10$$

- Investigate different ways of completing this addition statement using any 4 digits.
- You can use a digit more than once in each calculation.

- What about using any 6 digits?

$$\Box.\Box\Box + \Box.\Box\Box = 10$$

- What if the sum of the two decimal numbers was 9, 8, 7…1?

---

26 Running digits

• pencil and paper

- Look at the following calculations:

```
987 - 654 =
876 - 543 =
765 - 432 =
654 - 321 =
543 - 210 =
```

- Work out the answer to each calculation.
- Write about what you notice.

- What about these calculations?

```
9876 - 5432 =
8765 - 4321 =
7654 - 3210 =
```

• pencil and paper

27 999

- Choose a pair of 3-digit numbers.
- Subtract the smaller number from 999.
- Add this answer to the larger 3-digit number you chose.
- Look at your 4-digit answer. Separate the thousands digit from the hundreds, tens and units digits to get a 1-digit and a 3-digit number.
- Add together the 1-digit number and the 3-digit number.
- What is your answer?
- Now go back to the pair of 3-digit numbers you originally chose.
- Find the difference between these two numbers using your own method.
- What is your answer? What do you notice?
- Does this method always work?

```
578, 846
999 - 578 = 421
421 + 846 = 1267
1 + 267 = 268
846 - 578 = 268
```

- What would happen if you subtracted the smaller number from 1000?
- What if you choose a pair of 4-digit numbers and subtract the smaller number from 9999?

28 4-digit totals and differences

• pencil and paper

4 7 6 5

- Use the digits above to make 12 different 4-digit numbers between 5670 and 7560.
- Write the numbers in order.
- Find the pair of numbers with:
  - the smallest total
  - the largest total
  - the smallest difference
  - the largest difference.

- Altogether there are 24 different 4-digit numbers that can be made using the digits 4, 7, 6 and 5.
  Which pairs of numbers have:
  - the smallest total
  - the largest total
  - the smallest difference
  - the largest difference?

29 Equations

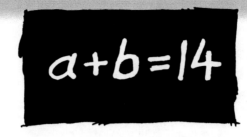

$$a + b = 14$$

- Look at the equation above.
- If *a* and *b* each stand for a different positive whole number, investigate possible values for *a* and *b*.
- If *a* and *b* stand for either a different positive or negative whole number, investigate possible values for *a* and *b*.

- What if the equation was this one?

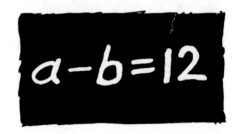

$$a - b = 12$$

30 Decimal clues

$\triangle$ and $\square$ stand for numbers.

The number $\triangle$ is between 10·5 and 11·8.

$$\triangle - \square = 7·9$$

- Investigate what $\triangle$ and $\square$ could be.

- What if:

$$\triangle - \square = 7·9$$ was replaced by $$\triangle + \square = 12·5$$

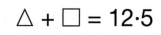

31 Opposites

- pencil and paper

- Draw a square.
- Write four numbers in the corners.
- Add the pairs of corner numbers.
- Write the totals between each pair of numbers.
- Now add the four totals together and write the final total inside the square.
- Do this several times.
- What do you notice?

- What if you found the difference between each pair of numbers?
- What if you drew a hexagon or an octagon?

32 Multiplication patterns

- calculator
- pencil and paper

- Work out the answers to these calculations.
- What patterns do you notice?
- Predict the answers to the next two calculations.
- Use a calculator to check your predictions.

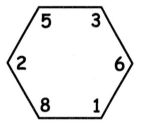

$5 \times 3 =$
$5 \times 33 =$
$5 \times 333 =$

- Now work out the answers to these calculations:
- What patterns do you notice?
- Predict the answers to the next two calculations.
- Use a calculator to check your predictions.

$5 \times 3 =$
$55 \times 3 =$
$555 \times 3 =$

- What patterns do you notice about each set of calculations?

- What if you started with a different times-table fact?

33 Decimal multiplications

• 1–9 digit cards
• pencil and paper

- Shuffle a set of 1–9 digit cards.
- Deal the top four cards and place them face up on the table.
- Arrange the four digits in the calculation below.

- How many different calculations can you make by rearranging your four digits?

- What if the calculation was:

34 Squares and multiplications

• pencil and paper

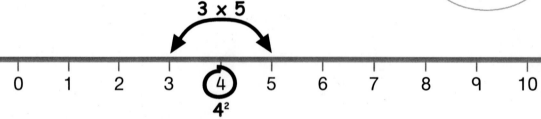

- Choose a number between 2 and 10.
- Multiply the number by itself.
- Now find the product of the two numbers that are one more and one less than your number.
- Do this for other numbers between 2 and 10.
- Write about what you notice.

- Does this work for numbers greater than 10?

35 Multiplying by 7

- Choose a 2-digit number and multiply the number by 7.
- Take the last two digits of your answer and multiply this new 2-digit number by 7.
- Keep doing this.
- What do you notice?

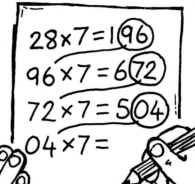

$28 \times 7 = 1\widehat{96}$
$96 \times 7 = 6\widehat{72}$
$72 \times 7 = 5\widehat{04}$
$04 \times 7 =$

- What if you multiply a 2-digit number by a different number?

---

36 Dividing multiples

- Write down all the multiples of 7 from 7 to 70.
- Now divide each of these multiples by 6.
- What patterns do you notice?
- Divide all the multiples of 7 by other numbers.
- What do you notice?

$7, 14, 21, \ldots$

$7 \div 6 = 1 r 1$
$14 \div 6 = 2 r 2$

- Write down all the multiples of 8 from 8 to 80 and divide each of these multiples by 7. What do you notice?
- What if you divided the multiples of 8 by other numbers?

37 Divisible by 11?

• pencil and paper

I have just discovered that when you reverse the digits of any 2-digit number to make a new number and find the total of the two numbers, your answer is always divisible by 11.

- Do you agree with Gary's statement?
- What happens if you use pairs of 3-digit, 4-digit or 5-digit numbers?
- What do you notice?

I wonder what I might discover if I found the difference between the two numbers?

- Investigate.

38 Using brackets

• pencil and paper

- Choose any four different digits between 1 and 9.
- Arrange the four digits in the calculation below and solve it.

$$(\boxed{} + \boxed{}) \times (\boxed{} + \boxed{}) =$$

- Make as many different calculations as you can by rearranging your four digits.

- What if the calculations were these?

$$(\boxed{} - \boxed{}) \times (\boxed{} - \boxed{}) =$$

$$(\boxed{} + \boxed{}) \times (\boxed{} - \boxed{}) =$$

$$(\boxed{} - \boxed{}) \times (\boxed{} + \boxed{}) =$$

39 Flow chart (1)

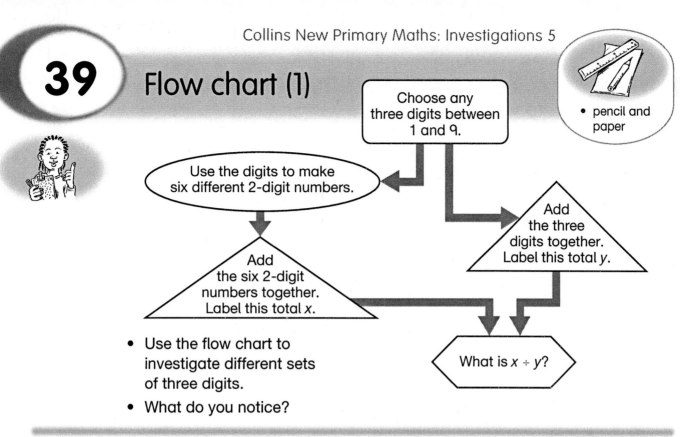

- pencil and paper

- Use the flow chart to investigate different sets of three digits.
- What do you notice?

- What if you used the three digits to make six different 3-digit numbers?

40 Flow chart (2)

- pencil and paper

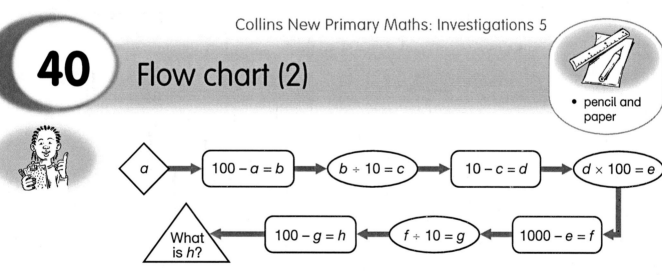

- Choose a 2-digit number. This number is a.
- Feed it into the flow chart.
- What number is h?
- Try this with other 2-digit numbers.
- What do you notice? Why?

- What would happen if a was a 1-digit or a 3-digit number?

41 Same digits different answer

• pencil and paper

- Choose any four different digits between 1 and 9.
- Write them down in any order.
- Use these digits in the exact order you have written them down to make a calculation using any of the four operations: +, −, × and ÷.
- You can use brackets if you wish.
- Investigate how many of the numbers from 1 to 100 you can make.

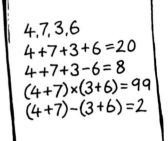

4, 7, 3, 6
$4+7+3+6 = 20$
$4+7+3-6 = 8$
$(4+7) \times (3+6) = 99$
$(4+7) - (3+6) = 2$

- What if you grouped the digits to make 2-digit or 3-digit numbers? You must still use the digits in the same order as before.

4, 7, 3, 6
$47 + 3 + 6 = 56$
$47 - 36 = 11$
$(47 \times 3) + 6 = 147$

✂

42 Missing digits

• pencil and paper

$$4 \;\square\; 8$$
$$\square\; 9 \;\square\; +$$
$$8\;5\;\square$$

$$\square\; 2 \;\square$$
$$3 \;\square\; 6 \;-$$
$$2\;6\;\square$$

$$\square\; 5$$
$$3 \;\square\; \times$$
$$3 \;\square\; 1\;5$$

$$7\;\square \div 6 = 1\;\square \; r \; \square$$

- Look at the four calculations above.
- Work out what each of the missing digits is.
- Is there more than one way?

- Make up some calculations like these for a friend to solve.

43 Coin percentages

• pencil and paper

$$\boxed{}\% \text{ of } £\bigcirc = \bigcirc p$$

• Write a 1-digit or 2-digit number in the box and any of these coins in the circles to complete the statement.

• You can only use each coin once for each statement.

• Here is one: $\boxed{10}\% \text{ of } £②= ㉒p$

• Investigate how many different statements you can make.

• What if you could use these notes and coins to complete either of these statements:

$$\boxed{}\% \text{ of } £\boxed{} = \bigcirc p$$

$$\boxed{}\% \text{ of } £\boxed{} = £\bigcirc$$

---

44 Pocket money

Week 1: 1p
Week 2: 2p
Week 3: 4p
Week 4: 8p
Week 5: …

• pencil and paper

• Would you be willing to take just one penny as pocket money this week as long as each week after that the amount of money would double?

• How much pocket money would you get in the 8th week?

• What about the 12th week? 15th week? 20th week? 24th week?

• How much pocket money would you have received altogether after the 24th week?

45 1 million steps

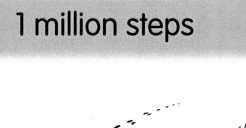

- measuring equipment
- pencil and paper

- Measure the length of your step.
- If you could take 1 million steps, how many kilometres would you travel?
- How many miles is this?

- How many steps would it take you to travel 10 km? 12 km? 20 miles? 50 miles?
- Choose some distances of your own and calculate how many steps you would need to take.

46 Sacks

- pencil and paper

30 kg 62 kg 51 kg 55 kg 43 kg 54 kg

- Each of these sacks contains either flour or sugar or rice.
- There is twice as much flour as sugar, and only one sack contains rice.
- Work out what each sack contains.

30 kg 4 kg 50 kg 6 kg 8 kg 7 kg 12 kg 7 kg 16 kg

- These sacks contain either flour, sugar, rice or pasta. There is three times as much flour as sugar, twice as much sugar as rice, and the same amount of rice as pasta. Work out what each sack contains.

47 The air we breathe

- clock or stopwatch
- pencil and paper

- On average you inhale 0·6 of a litre of air in one breath.
- How many breaths do you take in one minute?
- How much air is this?
- Estimate how much air you breathe in an hour.
- What about in a day?
- What about a week?

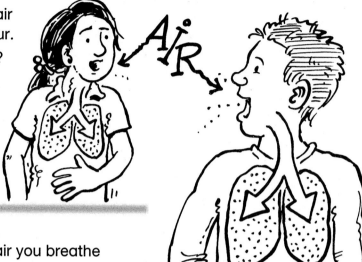

- Estimate how much air you breathe in a year.

---

48 When will it be?

- pencil and paper

- Write the date.
- Write the time to the nearest minute.
- When will it be:
  - 100 minutes from now?
  - 1000 minutes from now?
  - 100 hours from now?
  - 1000 hours from now?
  - 100 days from now?
  - 1000 days from now?

- How long is 1 million:
  - seconds in days?
  - minutes in weeks?
  - hours in years?

49 Shape areas

- square dotty paper
- pencil and paper

- These isosceles triangles each have a height of 3 units.
- Calculate the area of each triangle.

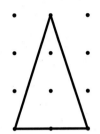
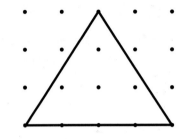

- Draw some other isosceles triangles that have a height of 3 units and investigate their areas.
- Investigate the areas of isosceles triangles with a height of 4 units, 5 units …

- What if you investigated the areas of other shapes of the same height?

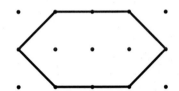

---

50 Expanding polygons

- squared paper
- ruler
- pencil

- Draw a rectangle. Label it 'A' and work out its area and perimeter.
- Draw shape 'A' again but with each side twice as long. Label it 'B' and work out its area and perimeter.
- Now draw shape 'A' again but this time with each side three times as long. Label it 'C' and work out its area and perimeter.
- What do you notice about the areas and perimeters of shapes A, B and C?

- Does this work for other polygons?

51 Matchstick shapes

- matchsticks
- pencil and paper

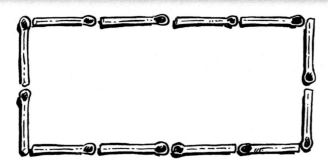

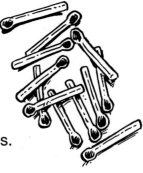

- Make a polygon using 12 matchsticks.
- All the angles of your polygon must be right angles.
- Make as many different polygons as you can.
- What is the perimeter of each shape?
- What is the area of each shape?

- What if you used 10, 18, 20… matchsticks?

---

52 Rectangles

- centimetre squared paper
- ruler
- scissors
- pencil and paper

- Using centimetre squared paper, draw 10 rectangles, each 2 cm × 4 cm, and cut them out.
- Join 6 of the rectangles together. How many different larger rectangles can you make?
- Here is one: ⟶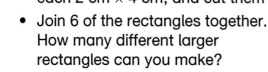
- Record your results.
- Now join 7 of the rectangles together. How many different larger rectangles can you make with a hole in them?
- Here is one: ⟶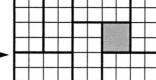
- Record your results.
- What about 2 holes?

- What if you used 8, 9 or 10 rectangles?

53 Shape meanings

- dictionary
- pencil and paper

> Polygon means 'many angles' in Greek.

- Investigate the meaning of each of the following prefixes:

dodeca- deca- hepta-

hexa- nona- octa- penta-

- Draw a shape to illustrate the meaning of each prefix.

- What does the suffix: '-hedron' mean?
- Which words do you know that have '-hedron' in them? What do they mean?

54 Diagonal, intersection, region

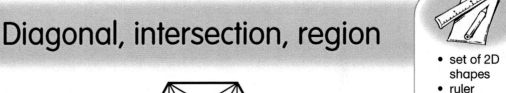

- set of 2D shapes
- ruler
- pencil and paper

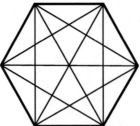

- A regular hexagon has 6 sides, 9 diagonals, 14 intersections and 24 regions.
- Draw an equilateral triangle, a square and a regular pentagon, heptagon and octagon.
- Investigate the number of sides, diagonals, intersections and regions in each shape.

- Can you predict how many sides, diagonals, intersections and regions a nonagon and a decagon would have?

55 How many squares?

 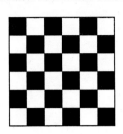

- A game uses a board with a 6 × 6 square grid.
- How many squares of all sizes are on the board?
- How many squares is this altogether?

There is one 6 x 6 square on this board.

- What if the game used a 10 × 10 square grid?
- Can you predict how many squares of all sizes are on a board of any size? What about the total number of squares?

---

56 Writing co-ordinates

- squared paper
- ruler
- a friend
- pencil and paper

To write capital 'E' I used the co-ordinates (4, 5), (1, 5), (1, 3), (3, 3), (1, 1) and (4, 1).

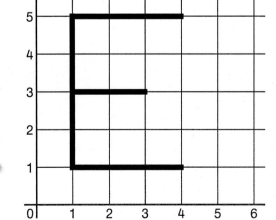

- Investigate which other capital letters you can write using co-ordinates.
- Write out the co-ordinates and give them to a friend to use. Can they write your letters?

- Which lower case letters can you write?
- Which digits can you write?

57 Capital rotation

- pencil and paper

- Capital N has rotational symmetry.
- Which other capital letters have rotational symmetry?

- What about the lower case letters?
- What about the digits?

---

58 Capital lines

- pencil and paper

- Investigate which capital letters have lines that are parallel to each other.
- Which capital letters have lines that are perpendicular to each other?
- Which capital letters have lines that are both parallel and perpendicular to each other?
- Present your results in a Venn diagram.

A
B C
D E F
G H I J
K L M N O
P Q R S T U
V W X Y Z

- What about the lower case letters?
- What about the digits?

59 Angle quadrilaterals

- squared paper
- ruler
- pencil and paper

- Draw a quadrilateral.
- Investigate the number of:
  - right angles
  - acute angles
  - obtuse angles
  - reflex angles.

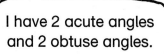

I have 3 acute angles and 1 reflex angle.

I have 2 acute angles and 2 obtuse angles.

- Try other shapes such as:
  - pentagons
  - hexagons
  - octagons.

---

60 Clock angles

- protractor
- pencil and paper

 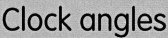

- If an analogue clock reads 12:10, what is the approximate size of the angle formed by the hands?
- What if it reads 2:25? 4:45?
- Choose other times to 5-minute intervals and work out the approximate size of the angles.
- Which of your angles are:
  - acute angles?
  - right angles?
  - obtuse angles?

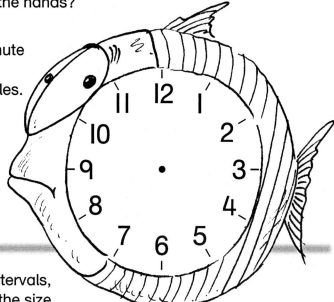

- Choose times to 1-minute intervals, such as 6:47, and measure the size of the angles.

Answers

Please note not all activities have answers.

Activity 14

171 tickets have one zero:
10, 20, 30, 40, 50, 60, 70, 80, 90,
101, 102, 103, 104, 105, 106,
107, 108, 109, 110, 120, 130,
140, 150, 160, 170, 180, 190,
201, 202, 203, 204, 205, 206,
207, 208, 209, 210, 220, 230,
240, 250, 260, 270, 280, 290,
301, 302, 303, 304, 305, 306,
307, 308, 309, 310, 320, 330,
340, 350, 360, 370, 380, 390,
401, 402, 403, 404, 405, 406,
407, 408, 409, 410, 420, 430,
440, 450, 460, 470, 480, 490,
501, 502, 503, 504, 505, 506,
507, 508, 509, 510, 520, 530,
540, 550, 560, 570, 580, 590,
601, 602, 603, 604, 605, 606,
607, 608, 609, 610, 620, 630,
640, 650, 660, 670, 680, 690,
701, 702, 703, 704, 705, 706,
707, 708, 709, 710, 720, 730,
740, 750, 760, 770, 780, 790,
801, 802, 803, 804, 805, 806,
807, 808, 809, 810, 820, 830,
840, 850, 860, 870, 880, 890,
901, 902, 903, 904, 905, 906,
907, 908, 909, 910, 920, 930,
940, 950, 960, 970, 980, 990

9 tickets have two zeros:
100, 200, 300, 400, 500, 600,
700, 800, 900

1 ticket has three zeros: 1000

Activity 15

The sum of each pair of diagonals always has a difference of 1.

Activity 16

The following numbers are multiples of 4 and multiples of 6:
12, 24, 36, 48, 60, 72, 84 and 96.
They are all multiples of 12.

Activity 17

$1 = 1^2 - 0^2$
$3 = 2^2 - 1^2$
$5 = 3^2 - 2^2$
$7 = 4^2 - 3^2$
$8 = 3^2 - 1^2$
$9 = 5^2 - 4^2$
$11 = 6^2 - 5^2$
$12 = 4^2 - 2^2$
$13 = 7^2 - 6^2$
$15 = 4^2 - 1^2$
$16 = 5^2 - 3^2$
$17 = 9^2 - 8^2$
$19 = 10^2 - 9^2$

$20 = 6^2 - 4^2$
$21 = 5^2 - 2^2$
$24 = 5^2 - 1^2$
$27 = 6^2 - 3^2$
$28 = 8^2 - 6^2$
$32 = 6^2 - 2^2$
$33 = 7^2 - 4^2$
$35 = 6^2 - 1^2$
$36 = 10^2 - 8^2$
$39 = 8^2 - 5^2$
$40 = 7^2 - 3^2$
$45 = 7^2 - 2^2$
$48 = 7^2 - 1^2$

Other answers are possible.

Activity 18

Each of the following numbers has 12 factors:
60: 1, 2, 3, 4, 5, 6, 10, 12, 15, 20, 30, 60.
72: 1, 2, 3, 4, 6, 8, 9, 12, 18, 24, 36, 72.
84: 1, 2, 3, 4, 6, 7, 12, 14, 21, 28, 42, 84.
90: 1, 2, 3, 5, 6, 9, 10, 15, 18, 30, 45, 90.
96: 1, 2, 3, 4, 6, 8, 12, 16, 24, 32, 48, 96.
They each have four common multiples: 1, 2, 3 and 6.

Activity 19

The following statements are true:
- The sum of three even numbers is always even.
- The difference between one odd and one even number is always odd.

The following statements are false:
- The sum of three odd numbers is always even. (The sum of three odd numbers is always odd.)

- The difference between two odd or two even numbers is always odd. (The difference between two odd or two even numbers is always even)

Activity 20

$\frac{1}{4}, \frac{2}{4}\left(\frac{1}{2}\right), \frac{3}{4}$

$\frac{1}{5}, \frac{2}{5}, \frac{3}{5}, \frac{4}{5}$

$\frac{1}{6}, \frac{2}{6}\left(\frac{1}{3}\right), \frac{3}{6}\left(\frac{1}{2}\right), \frac{4}{6}\left(\frac{2}{3}\right), \frac{5}{6}$

$\frac{1}{7}, \frac{2}{7}, \frac{3}{7}, \frac{4}{7}, \frac{5}{7}, \frac{6}{7}$

$\frac{1}{8}, \frac{2}{8}\left(\frac{1}{4}\right), \frac{3}{8}, \frac{4}{8}\left(\frac{1}{2}\right), \frac{5}{8}, \frac{6}{8}\left(\frac{3}{4}\right), \frac{7}{8}$

$\frac{1}{9}, \frac{2}{9}, \frac{3}{9}\left(\frac{1}{3}\right), \frac{4}{9}, \frac{5}{9}, \frac{6}{9}\left(\frac{2}{3}\right), \frac{7}{9}, \frac{8}{9}$

$\frac{1}{10}, \frac{2}{10}\left(\frac{1}{5}\right), \frac{3}{10}, \frac{4}{10}\left(\frac{2}{5}\right), \frac{5}{10}\left(\frac{1}{2}\right), \frac{6}{10}\left(\frac{3}{5}\right), \frac{7}{10}, \frac{8}{10}\left(\frac{4}{5}\right), \frac{9}{10}$

Fifths and sevenths (and elevenths, thirteenths…) cannot be reduced. All these fraction families have prime numbers as their denominators.

Activity 21

The following pairs of improper fractions have a denominator of 3 and total:
- 4: $\frac{6}{3} + \frac{6}{3}$
- 5: $\frac{9}{3} + \frac{6}{3}$
- 6: $\frac{9}{3} + \frac{9}{3}$
- 7: $\frac{12}{3} + \frac{9}{3}$
- 8: $\frac{15}{3} + \frac{9}{3}$
- 9: $\frac{15}{3} + \frac{12}{3}$
- 10: $\frac{15}{3} + \frac{15}{3}$

Other answers are possible.

Activity 22

7 calculations have an answer with exactly 2 decimal places:
$1 \div 4 = 0·25$
$2 \div 8 = 0·25$
$3 \div 4 = 0·75$
$5 \div 4 = 1·25$
$6 \div 8 = 0·75$
$7 \div 4 = 1·75$
$9 \div 4 = 2·25$

In each calculation, the divisor is either 4 or 8.
All the answers have decimals of either ·25 or ·75.

Activity 23

The percent of numbers on a
1 to 100 number square that are:
– odd numbers is 50%
– multiples of 3 is 33%
– multiples of 2 and 5 is 10%
– square numbers is 10%
– factors of 36 is 9%

Activity 25

Accept any pair of decimal
numbers with one decimal place
that total 10, e.g. 2·4 + 7·6 and
3·5 + 6·5.

Activity 26

All the calculations have an
answer of 333.

Activity 27

The answers are the same. This
method always works.

Activity 28

The 12 different 4-digit numbers
between 5670 and 7560 that
can be made using the digits
4, 5, 6 and 7 are, in order:
5674, 5746, 5764, 6457, 6475,
6547, 6574, 6745, 6754, 7456,
7465 and 7546.
The pair of numbers with the
smallest total is:
5674 + 5746 = 11 420
The pair of number with the
largest total is:
7465 + 7546 = 15 011
The pairs of numbers with the
smallest difference are:
6754 – 6745 = 9 and
7465 – 7456 = 9.
The pair of number with the
largest difference is:
7546 – 5674 = 1872.

Activity 29

If a and b each stands for a
different positive whole number,
either a or b could stand for:

0 and 14	4 and 10
1 and 13	5 and 9
2 and 12	6 and 8
3 and 11	

If a and b stand for either a
different positive or negative
whole number, accept any
calculation that has an answer
of 14, e.g.

-1 + 15	20 + -6
-2 + 16	18 + -4
-15 + 29	36 + -22

Activity 30

△ □	△ □
10·6 – 2·7	11·2 – 3·3
10·7 – 2·8	11·3 – 3·4
10·8 – 2·9	11·4 – 3·5
10·9 – 3	11·5 – 3·6
11 – 3·1	11·6 – 3·7
11·1 – 3·2	11·7 – 3·8

Also, accept answers where
children have used tenths and
hundredths, e.g.

△ □	△ □
10·51 – 2·61	10·52 – 2·62

Activity 31

The sum of both opposite pairs,
i.e. 36, (11 + 15 and 13 + 13)
is exactly half the total of the
four numbers together,
i.e. 52 (11 + 15 + 13 + 13).

Activity 32

$5 \times 3 = 15$
$5 \times 33 = 165$
$5 \times 333 = 1665$
Predictions:
$5 \times 3333 = 16665$
$5 \times 33333 = 166665$

$5 \times 3 = 15$
$55 \times 3 = 165$
$555 \times 3 = 1665$
Predictions:
$5555 \times 3 = 16665$
$55555 \times 3 = 166665$

The digits that make up the
answer to the first multiplication
fact, i.e. 15, are the first and last
digits in the subsequent
calculations. The middle digits in
the subsequent calculations are
the same digit, i.e. 6, repeated.
The answers to both sets of
calculations are the same.

Activity 33

24 different calculations can be
made.

Activity 34

When a number is squared,
e.g. $4^2 = 16$, the answer is always
one more than the product of the
two numbers that are one more
and one less than the number,
i.e. $3 \times 5 = 15$.

Activity 35

After four calculations, you get
back to your original
2-digit number, therefore creating
a loop, e.g.

$28 \times 7 = 196$	$55 \times 7 = 385$
$96 \times 7 = 672$	$85 \times 7 = 595$
$72 \times 7 = 504$	$95 \times 7 = 665$
$04 \times 7 = 28$	$65 \times 7 = 455$

Activity 36

When dividing the multiples of 7
by 6, a pattern occurs with the
remainders, i.e. 1, 2, 3, 4, 5, 0, 1,
2, 3, 4…

$7 \div 6 = 1 \, r \, 1$	$42 \div 6 = 7$
$14 \div 6 = 2 \, r \, 2$	$49 \div 6 = 8 \, r \, 1$
$21 \div 6 = 3 \, r \, 3$	$56 \div 6 = 9 \, r \, 2$
$28 \div 6 = 4 \, r \, 4$	$63 \div 6 = 10 \, r \, 3$
$35 \div 6 = 5 \, r \, 5$	$70 \div 6 = 11 \, r \, 4$

Similar patterns with the
remainders also occur when
dividing the multiples of 7 by
other numbers, e.g.

$7 \div 5 = 1 \, r \, 2$	$42 \div 5 = 8 \, r \, 2$
$14 \div 5 = 2 \, r \, 4$	$49 \div 5 = 9 \, r \, 4$
$21 \div 5 = 4 \, r \, 1$	$56 \div 5 = 11 \, r \, 1$
$28 \div 5 = 5 \, r \, 3$	$63 \div 5 = 12 \, r \, 3$
$35 \div 5 = 7$	$70 \div 5 = 14$

$7 \div 4 = 1 \, r \, 3$	$42 \div 4 = 10 \, r \, 2$
$14 \div 4 = 3 \, r \, 2$	$49 \div 4 = 12 \, r \, 1$
$21 \div 4 = 5 \, r \, 1$	$56 \div 4 = 14$
$28 \div 4 = 7$	$63 \div 4 = 15 \, r \, 3$
$35 \div 4 = 8 \, r \, 3$	$70 \div 4 = 17 \, r \, 2$

$7 \div 3 = 2 \, r \, 1$	$42 \div 3 = 14$
$14 \div 3 = 4 \, r \, 2$	$49 \div 3 = 16 \, r \, 1$
$21 \div 3 = 7$	$56 \div 3 = 18 \, r \, 2$
$28 \div 3 = 9 \, r \, 1$	$63 \div 3 = 21$
$35 \div 3 = 11 \, r \, 2$	$70 \div 3 = 23 \, r \, 1$

$7 \div 2 = 3 \, r \, 1$ $42 \div 2 = 21$
$14 \div 2 = 7$ $49 \div 2 = 24 \, r \, 1$
$21 \div 2 = 10 \, r \, 1$ $56 \div 2 = 28$
$28 \div 2 = 14$ $63 \div 2 = 31 \, r \, 1$
$35 \div 2 = 17 \, r \, 1$ $70 \div 2 = 35$

Activity 37

Gary is right. When you reverse the digits of any 2-digit number to make a new number and find the total of the two numbers, the answer is always divisible by 11, e.g.
$87 + 78 = 165 \div 11 = 15$
$49 + 94 = 143 \div 11 = 13$
This only applies to numbers with an even number of digits, i.e. pairs of 2-digit, 4-digit, 6-digit… numbers.

Activity 39

The final answer is always 22.

Activity 40

a and *h* are always the same numbers. This is because all the operations within the flow chart cancel each other out, so that the end number (*h*) is always the same as the start number (*a*).

Activity 42

```
 458      624        9 5
 397 +    356 -      3 7 ×
 ─────    ─────     ─────
 855      268       3515
```

$75 \div 6 = 12 \, r \, 3$

Other answers are possible.

Activity 43

$25\% \times £2 = 50p$ $20\% \times £1 = 20p$
$10\% \times £2 = 20p$ $10\% \times £1 = 10p$
$5\% \times £2 = 10p$ $5\% \times £1 = 5p$
$1\% \times £2 = 2p$ $2\% \times £1 = 2p$
$50\% \times £1 = 50p$ $1\% \times £1 = 1p$

Activity 44

You would receive £1.28 pocket money in the 8th week, £20.48 in the 12th week, £163.84 in the 15th week, £5242.88 in the 20th week and £83 886.08 in the 24th week.

Activity 45

Answers will vary depending on the size of individual children's step, however if a child's step is 25 cm, then they would travel about 250 kilometres in 1 million steps, which is about 156 miles.

Activity 46

Flour: 51 kg, 55 kg, 62 kg
Sugar: 30 kg, 54 kg
Rice: 43 kg

Activity 47

If a child takes, on average, 10 breaths in one minute, then they inhale 6 litres in a minute. That is 360 litres in an hour, 8640 litres in a day and 60 480 litres in a week.

Activity 48

When will it be:
– 100 minutes from now? (add 1 hour and 40 minutes)
– 1000 minutes from now? (add 16 hours and 40 minutes)
– 100 hours from now? (add 4 days and 4 hours)
– 1000 hours from now? (add 41 days and 16 hours)
– 100 days from now? (teacher)
– 1000 days from now? (add 2 years and 270 days or 271 days if one of the years is a leap year)

Activity 50

The area of shape 'B' is four times that of shape 'A'. The area of shape 'C' is nine times that of shape 'A'.

The perimeter of shape 'B' is twice that of shape 'A'. The perimeter of shape 'C' is three times that of shape 'A'.

Activity 51

Each shape will have a perimeter of 12 units. The areas of the different shapes will vary.

Activity 53

dodeca- 12   hepta- 7
deca- 10   hexa- 6
nona- 9   penta- 5
octa- 8

Activity 54

An equilateral triangle has 3 sides, 0 diagonals, 0 intersections and 1 region.
A square has 4 sides, 2 diagonals, 1 intersection and 4 regions.
A pentagon has 5 sides, 5 diagonals, 5 intersections and 11 regions.
A heptagon has 7 sides, 14 diagonals, 35 intersections and 50 regions.
A octagon has 8 sides, 20 diagonals, 70 intersections and 91 regions.

Activity 55

1×1 square = 36
2×2 square = 25
3×3 square = 16
4×4 square = 9
5×5 square = 4
6×6 square = 1
Total = 91

Activity 57

The letters H, I, N, O, S, X and Z all have rotational symmetry.

Activity 58

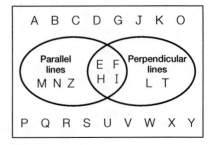

Activity 60

12:10: 60° (acute angle)
2:25: 90° (right angle)
4:45: 150° (obtuse angle)

Software information

IMPORTANT, PLEASE READ CAREFULLY – LICENCE AGREEMENT

This licence agreement ("the Licence") is a legal contract between HarperCollins*Publishers* Ltd ("Publisher"); and you the Licensee ("Licensee") which shall mean the relevant partnership, corporate body, trust charity, school, educational establishment or any other body on whose behalf the purchaser has acquired the work. In consideration of your agreeing to abide by the terms of this Licence, the Publisher hereby grants the Licensee a non-exclusive, non-transferable licence to use the software, documentation and contents of the CD-ROM ("the CD ROM") in the UK on the terms of this Licence. By installing and using the CD-ROM, you the Licensee agree to the terms of this Licence. If you the Licensee do not agree to the terms of this Licence we are unwilling to licence this software to you and you should not use or install the CD-ROM.

RESTRICTIONS ON USE

Any Licensee which is an educational institution may print and edit unlimited copies of the Microsoft Word™ and PDF document files ("Files") contained on the CD-ROM for use exclusively within that institution, and is granted a licence to host and store the Files on their computer network and/or communal hard-drive, which may be accessed and printed solely by the Licensee's employees and pupils over an intranet/school web page only. This Licence does not grant the Licensee a licence to make the Files available via any public domain site or for duplicate copies of the Files, edited Files or the CD-ROM in any format to be made for the purpose of loaning, donating renting or selling to any other institution without the permission of the Publisher. Nor does the Licence allow for any commercial purpose including but not limited to altering, cropping, printing or other treatment of all or any part of any artwork, images, sound, music, or text held on the CD-ROM and the rental, lending, networking, resale, remote access and inclusion on a bulletin board of the CD-ROM or any of its content. There is no right, by virtue of this purchase, for the Licensee to copy, adapt or make copies of an adaptation in connection with the CD-ROM, except as expressly permitted by law. Notwithstanding the foregoing, in the event that the Licensee is a school or other educational establishment, the Licensee shall have the right to make one back-up copy only of the CD-ROM. All moral rights of artists and all other contributors to the CD-ROM are hereby asserted and you acknowledge that all intellectual property rights in the CD-ROM throughout the world belong to the Publisher, that rights in the CD-ROM are licensed (not assigned) to you, and that you have no rights in, or to, the CD-ROM other than the right to use them in accordance with the terms of this Licence. The Licence referred to is deemed to take effect when the CD-ROM installation routine is invoked. Licensee acknowledges that the CD-ROM may not be free of errors or bugs and that the existence of any minor errors shall not constitute a breach of this Licence. The CD-ROM has not been developed for general use and it is the Licensee's responsibility to ensure the facilities and functions of the CD-ROM meet their requirements.

All other titles, obligations and liabilities of the Publishers, including but not limited to consequential loss, loss of profits, or any economic loss arising from the use, the inability to use, or any defect in the CD-ROM are excluded in so far as permitted by UK law. This Agreement and licence are specific to the Licence and all rights not expressly provided herein are reserved to the Publishers and no rights of any nature may be assigned, licensed or made over to any third party. This agreement is subject to English law and the jurisdiction of the English courts.

For information on technical support, please go to: www.collinseducation.com/ithelp